Brigitte Sedlaczek

ARCHAEOLOGY OF
THE *Maltese Islands*

Distributed by:

PROGRESS PRESS Co. Ltd.
341 ST PAUL ST VALLETTA
Tel: (+356)241464 - Fax: (+356)237150

Published by:

MP GRAPHIC FORMULA

Roma Italia

Introduction

The Maltese archipelago, or Il Gzejjer Maltin in the local language, is situated almost exactly at the centre of the Mediterranean, between the coasts of Sicily and North Africa. It lies 95 km from Sicily and 290 km from Tunisia. The archipelago consists of two main islands, Malta and Gozo together with the smaller islands of Comino, Filfla and Cominotto. Its central position at the narrowest point of the Mediterranean facilitates contact between East and West and between Europe and Africa. For this reason, Malta has always been of great strategic importance.

From a geological point of view, the Maltese islands form part of the continent of Europe and are formed of sedimentary limestone derived from an accumulation of fossilised shells. There are two types of limestone - coralline limestone, which is hard and compact, and globigerina, which is soft and easily worked. The latter is still the most widely-used building material on the islands.

There are no mountains on the islands. The highest points are on Malta, in the hills south of Dingli which reach a height of 258 metres, and on Gozo, where one point reaches 194 metres.

On the eastern half of the island of Malta, from Mosta to Zejtun, the land gently ridges, scored by several dry riverbeds (wied in Maltese). These valleys, where water flows during the winter rains, have always been used for agriculture. Going eastwards from the south, the coastline is indented with bays, inlets and fjords.

The coastline of the south-west is rocky and steep with no landing-places for boats.

The north-western part of the island slopes towards the sea in a series of well-defined steps. The crests reach a height of 150 m, while the valleys drop as low as sea level. The coastline is heavily indented. As the water table in the valleys is not very deep, the land is extremely fertile. The northernmost point of the island is a rocky platform in the form of a fish tail.

The terrain of Gozo is less characteristic.

The island lies to the north-west of Malta and rises only a few tens of metres above sea level.

The highest point is found at the cliffs of Ta' Cenc. During the Ice Age, about 250,000 years ago, the Maltese archipelago formed part of the European continent and was joined by land to Sicily and Italy. The formation of glaciers had resulted in a notable drop in sea levels. As they melted, however, the sea level rose and the landbridge which had joined Malta to Sicily vanished. One result of this was to trap on the islands many species of animal which no longer exist there today. Evidence of this can be seen in the remains and skeletons of elephants, hippopotami, deer, bears and others, found in the cave of Ghar Dalam.

The Neolithic Period

The islands appear to have been covered with woods and rivers during the Neolithic Period. Today, however, both woods and rivers have disappeared. At the end of the 6th millennium BC, when the Maltese islands were already separated from the European mainland, Stone Age man began to make his appearance, arriving by boat from Sicily. These people were farmers and brought with them their animals and tools. Almost the entire island of Malta was settled, with the exception of the central zone and the Marfa Ridge in the north.

Quarrying and the use of stone have made it difficult to find remains which would throw some light on antiquity. Luckily, however, some Neolithic finds have been made in the area of Luqa and near the quarry which lies close to the airport.

Systematic archaeological research, documented and ratified, began only recently. On the 28th February 1991, The Times carried an article on the discovery of a Stone Age cave at Ghajn Abdul, on Gozo, which had risked being lost for ever.

The Neolithic Era in Malta, also known as the Temple Period, can be divided into several phases. The first phase is the Ghar Dalam culture (beginning in 5000 BC), named after a cave situated near Birzebbuga on the south-eastern coast. This phase influenced by south-east Sicilian Stentinello culture which is characterised by impressed ware and also by the working of stone. The latter was a real industry, using obsidian from Lipari and Pantelleria.

There follows the Skorba phase, from Skorba near Mgarr in the north-western Malta. This phase is divided into two groups - Grey Skorba and Red Skorba, names derived from the colours of the ainted pottery of the period, one grey without decoration, the other red, with decorative incisions. The discovery of figurines with undoubtedly feminine attributes suggests an ancestral religious worship of a propitiatory fertility goddess. Female idols, though, both in clay and in ivory, are well-known even in the Palaeolithic Era (25000-18000 BC), an example being a clay "Venus" with enormous breasts found in the Czech Republic.

The Megalithic Temples

Considering its size, Malta boasts one of the highest concentrations of megalithic temples still in existence. Such a wealth of temples leads us to suppose that they were necessary in order to accommodate worshippers from abroad. Without doubt, these megalithic temples are Malta's most remarkable monuments. They are thought to be the oldest open-air religious constructions in the world. By comparison, the Pyramid of Cheops (2500 BC), Stonehenge (c.2300 BC) and even the earliest Minoan palaces on Crete (c.1800 BC) are all more recent than the Maltese temples.

Scientifically precise dating of monuments and ancient objects can be carried out in several ways, the safest and most important of which is radiocarbon, or carbon-14, dating. While studying the composition of carbon-14, the American chemist and physicist Willard Frank Libby (1908-80) discovered a way to establish the date of very old organic matter, for example plants and tree rings. He was awarded the Nobel prize for Chemistry in 1960 for his work.

The megalithic temples signal the second period in Maltese prehistory, and can be divided into several phases beginning with the Zebbug phase (from 4100 BC). There is a new wave of arrivals, perhaps from Sardinia, and new settlements are established. There are tombs carved from solid rock near Zebbug and also near Xemxija. The pottery of this period is grey or yellow with red or white incrustations.

This leads into the Mgarr phase (from about 3800 BC), which lasts only a short time. Its pottery is quite distinctive, with curved decorations and bands incised before firing. The tombs are horse-shoe-shaped and are carved out of the rock, as at Xemxija near St. Paul's Bay.

Next comes the Ggantija phase on the island of Gozo (from 3600 BC). This phase marks the beginning of temples built with enormous blocks of stone, as can be clearly seen at Ggantija, Ta' Hagrat, Skorba, Mnajdra and Tarxien. These were temples dedicated to fertility cults and the worship of "fat divinities", female figures with wide hips and large breasts.

The contemporary painter and sculptor Fernando Botero (b. Colombia, 1932) may well have been influenced by these obese figures. However, looking closely at some of the statues from over the whole Temple Period, whether they be seated, standing or above all lying, it can be seen that there are not only fat female figures but fat male figures too, similar to modern-day Japanese Sumo wrestlers. More study is necessary, though, before their meaning can be fully understood. The pottery decorations of this phase are more complex, with curves and coloured hatching.

After the Ggantija phase comes the Saflieni phase (from about 3300 BC). The name Saflieni comes from the Hypogeum of Hal Saflieni at Paola. A hypogeum is an underground construction, used principally for burials, but also for religious worship. The Hypogeum of Hal Saflieni was discovered by chance during excavation work for a water cistern. The famous Maltese archaeologist Sir Themistocles Zammit directed the dig which lasted six years. The Hypogeum is an important monument, built over three subterranean levels from 3 to 10 metres and laid out like a labyrinth. It resembles an underground version of the megalithic temples. Its cubicles, rooms, passages and steps were carved out of the limestone and decorated with frescoes. This hypogeum was used both as a religious site and a place of burial, a fact evidenced by the discovery of around 7,000 skeletons. During this phase, the first double-axis temples appear, like those at Skorba, Mgarr and Tarxien. The ceramic ware is noted for spiral decorations and we have the first appearance of trilithic altars, which use a special arrangement of stone blocks. At this point we reach the start of construction on the Hagar Qim and Mnajdra temples, built on the southern coast of Malta, near the sea.

The final phase of the second prehistoric epoch in Malta is the Tarxien phase (from 3000 BC) which is noted for the building of the Central Temple of Tarxien. The temple complex of Tarxien is situated quite near to the Hypogeum. The most important discovery of Neolithic artefacts in Malta was made at these temples during the First World War. They are considered of such importance for this period due to the excellent state of preservation, and can be found on display at the National Museum of Archaeology in Valletta. The Tarxien complex contains four temples. The first dates to the Ggantija phase. It is somewhat smaller than the others and lies a short distance away. This phase saw the completion of Ggantija, Hagar Qim and Mnajdra and an extension of the Hypogeum. The pottery of this period is decorated with spirals and the sculptures are generally of human figurines. A high level of civilisation is evident in this period together with strong religious power. As far as food is concerned, we know that oil and wine were already being produced.

The Bronze Age

The development of this last phase of the Temple period remains today as mysterious as its extinction. At the end of the period of Tarxien Culture, around 2500 BC, the construction of temples suddenly ceases and there is no further trace of the population. There are no signs of any natural disasters, as, for example, those which befell the Minoan culture. The possible causes are various - famine, epidemics or invasions - but the fact remains that a gap of about 500 years follows until traces of a new culture are found. Around the year 2000 BC, new settlers arrived, bringing another culture to Malta - Bronze Age culture. The new arrivals were not, though, as highly developed in cultural and technical matters and the temples went to ruin. Practically the only evidence of their impact, in fact, is a necropolis where the dead were cremated, at the great Tarxien site. These people used bronze weapons and tools, a fact which could indicate a certain relationship with the Bronze Age warrior cultures of Greece, Southern Italy and Sicily.

There is no evidence of any settlements in this first phase of Bronze Age culture, also known as the Tarxien Cemetery culture. The only constructions which can be attributed to this people are the dolmens which abound on both main islands.

The second phase of the Bronze Age is what is known as the Borg in-Nadur phase. This culture, which existed from about 1500 - 700 BC, takes its name from a fortified village in the area of Marsaxlokk and is characterised by an apparent need for defence. The name Borg in-Nadur, in fact, means "hilltop fort", and the village consists of a monumental Neolithic complex and Bronze Age settlement. The pottery of the period is characterised by deep zigzag lines which are generally filled with a white paste.

The last phase of the Bronze Age on Malta is known as the Bahrija phase (c.900 - 700 BC). The new colonisers probably arrived from Southern Italy (Calabria, possibly). In the course of this phase, the new arrivals produced dark grey or black pottery decorated with geometric patterns, zigzagging or twisting lines. The patterns were created by scoring the clay itself and filling the grooves with a white paste.

The Cart-Ruts

One feature which has yet to be fully explained are the so-called "cart-ruts", tracks carved or worn down in the ground, probably by carts or sleds. One of the sites with the highest concentration of these tracks, Misrah Ghar il-Kbir, is also known as Clapham Junction, a name bestowed by an English visitor who compared the ruts to the railway tracks at the train station of that name on the outskirts of London.

The ruts are to be found in many parts of Malta and Gozo and are almost always near quarries. There is as yet no evidence to link these quarries with the carved tracks. In fact, the precise function of the ruts has still to be established; opinion ranges from the transportation of stone blocks to a system of irrigation. As far as their age is concerned, they can almost certainly be dated to around 1500-1000 BC, in the late Bronze Age.

The fact that there are no ruts near the Neolithic temples confirms that they first appeared in a later phase to that of the temples themselves.

The Birth of History: The Phoenicians

Around the year 900 BC, the Phoenicians landed on Malta. The island's strategic position at the centre of the Mediterranean offered an ideal port of call to the Phoenicians for their commercial trading. It is perhaps thanks to its natural harbours that Malta was given the name Mlt, meaning "place of refuge".

The Phoenicians were a people of sailors, moving around continually from Palestine to Gibraltar, always on the lookout for wood needed in the construction or repair of their ships. It is therefore presumed that the deforestation of Malta was their handiwork. There have been hopes of finding some written documents at digs on various Phoenician sites, given that they were literate; however, the results to date have been few and far between. From their time on the island there remain the rock-hewn tombs of Siggiewi, Paola and Mdina. In the 1960s, Italian archaeologists discovered Tas-Silg, an important religious site dedicated to the goddess Astarte, which lies on the south-eastern coast overlooking Marsaxlokk harbour. Several place-names in Malta owe their origin to Phoenician names, for example Marsaxlokk and Marsaskala.

The Carthaginians

The successors of the Phoenicians were the Carthaginians, Phoenician colonists from Carthage. From the mid-6th century BC onward, the period is known as the Punic period, from the name given to this people by the Romans - the Poeni.

They dominated the Western Mediterranean, making Malta into a bulwark against the Greeks who were trying to expand their influence. This is the reason for the almost total absence of traces of Hellenic culture in Malta. Thanks again to the Carthaginians, the islands became a strategic base for commercial contacts with the East, proof of which can be seen in the Egyptian scarabs found among tomb furnishings.

Nonetheless, Malta continued to maintain strong cultural and commercial links with the Greek city-colonies of Sicily, Magna Græcia and Libya. Artefacts found in 4th-3rd century BC tombs resemble those from the necropolises of Leptis Magna in Libya.

In many places, both on Malta and on Gozo, Phoenician-type tombs have been found. Most archaeological discoveries, in fact, have come from necropolises, which have provided an enormous amount of material. The majority were inter-ment chambers with an entrance shaft and one or two chambers cut from the rock. The oldest imported objects (for example, Proto-Corinthian artefacts) come from tombs in the area of Rabat, Mtarfa and Dingli. For information on the nature and scope of the Punic sanctuary of Ras il-Wardija on the island of Gozo, the reader is referred to P. Mingazzini (RSTF 4, 1976, p.159-166). It is a stone block edifice, an open-air sanctuary which is recognisably Punic due to the presence of a graffito in the form of a "sign of Tanit", engraved on a wall. In fact, there are many other symbolic graffiti. It is comparable to a cave in the vicinity of Tyre (a rich, ancient Phoenician city in modern-day Lebanon) which is thought, with a good degree of certainty, to be the religious site mentioned in a Greek inscription in which the author gives thanks to Aphrodite. The Phoenician and Carthaginian period comes to a close with the First Punic War.

The Romans in Malta

As a step in their ongoing confrontation with the Carthaginians, the Romans, under the consul Tiberius Sempronius Longus, conquered Malta and Gozo in 218 BC, at the start of the Second Punic War, also known as Hannibal's War (see Livy, XXI.51).

It was from here that they planned their conquest of Carthage. The Maltese population were not hostile to the Romans, who established their capital at Melita on the site of the present-day Mdina and which, under the Roman Empire, was promoted to the status of municipium. During the Roman occupation, Malta produced honey, linen and olive oil for trading purposes. Honey, in fact, became the most important export of all, a fact noted even by Cicero. It may well even have given the island its name - Melita/Malta.

After the Battle of Zama (North Africa) in 202 BC which brought the Second Punic War to a close, the Maltese islands became part of the Roman province of Sicily.

The destruction of Carthage in 146 BC saw the rise of Malta to such heights as to become the base for commercial traffic with the northern coasts of Africa. Despite the long presence of the Romans in Malta, though, the Maltese people did not come under the influence of Roman culture and even continued to speak their Punic dialect. The fact that the Punic language survived the Roman domination is illustrated in an episode in the life of St. Paul. He was shipwrecked on the north-eastern coast of Malta in about AD 58 and remained on the island for about three months. According to St. Luke in the Acts of the Apostles (27:39 - 28:10), Paul described the people of the island as "barbaroi", meaning "people who speak a strange tongue", i.e. neither Latin nor Greek, both of which were well known to Paul and Luke.

Another interesting description of Malta comes from the Frenchman Jean Quintin in 1534 who says, among other things, "Malta fell into the hands of the Romans at the same time as Sicily, after which time it has always had the same laws and the same government".

As far as housing at the time of the Romans is concerned, there is evidence from the historian Diodorus Siculus (1st century BC) (v.12,2) who says "and the dwellings on the island are most noteworthy, being built in an ambitious manner, with cornices and decorated with stuccoes of uncommon skill". Diodorus further praises the work of the Maltese artisans, above all their weaving skills.

On the west coast, not far from Mgarr, near the bays of Ghajn Tuffieha and Gnejna, there are ruins of public baths in a reasonable state of repair. There have also been many findings of coins minted on Malta and Gozo which are indispensable for the purposes of dating. The coins are now housed in the various museums on the islands.

The most significant example, however, of Roman building is the villa, or domus, of Rabat. Rabat is in the south-west corner of the island. One half of the villa lies over the Roman town of Melita, while the other half lies above the Palaeochristian catacombs. The Roman villa was excavated in 1881 and transformed into a museum in 1924. Its foundations would indicate a rather opulent townhouse, rather than a country villa. The atrium is surrounded by a Doric peristyle which has a fabulous mosaic. The other rooms are the vestibule and the triclinium, both decorated with beautiful mosaics, in a rather less well-conserved condition. On display at the villa-museum are a number of artefacts from the Palaeochristian catacombs and Punic tombs, together with ceramic and glass ware

(vases, etc.), marble architectural fragments, the base of a statue complete with inscription of the Roman municipium, busts of Roman emperors, including the colossal head of the Emperor Claudius (AD 41-54). There are even Arab tombstones! In 1747 an important Latin inscription was discovered in the town of Mdina. The text refers to structural elements of a tetrastyle temple dedicated to Apollo, god of the sun. Its builder or restorer was a Roman patron of the arts. The Carthaginian tradition of burials in subterranean chambers carved out of the rock continued right up to the end of the Roman period, when the use of catacombs was introduced by the early Christians. From existing inscriptions, it is known that Punic religious practices were tolerated even under Roman domination. Some trustworthy written sources dealing with the Carthaginian and Roman periods are the writings of Diodorus Siculus (c.80-20 BC), Livy (59 BC - AD 17) and the Graeco-Egyptian astronomer and mathematician Ptolemy (c. AD 85-160). With the fall of the Roman Empire, the Maltese islands were abandoned by the Romans and came into the possession of the Vandals, who conquered North Africa. In AD 395, the Roman Empire was split into the Western Roman Empire (Rome) and the Eastern Roman Empire (Byzantium). When the general Belisarius conquered Malta and Sicily in AD 533 on behalf of the Byzantine emperor Justinian, the Maltese archipelago fell under the influence of the Eastern Empire.

Paleochristian Period

The Palaeochristian, or Early Christian, period begins during the Roman period. The term "Palaeochristian" is used to indicate the first centuries of the Christian era, up to about the 6th century AD. There is no true Palaeochristian style but rather a late classical style using Christian symbols. The style is generally found on the walls of catacombs, in frescoes showing biblical scenes and later also on sarcophagi. Only at a much later date, when the Edict of Constantine in AD 313 conceded freedom of worship throughout the empire, do we find Early Christian basilicas with colonnaded naves, which were later to develop into true basilicas and churches. Examples of the Palaeochristian era are found above all in tombs, hypogea and catacombs.

GEOLOGICAL ERA	PHASE	DATES
NEOLITHIC	GHAR DALAM	5000 - 4500
	GREY SKORBA	4500 - 4400
	RED SKORBA	4400 - 4100
MEGALITHIC TEMPLE PERIOD	ZEBBUG	4100 - 3800
	MGARR	3800 - 3600
	GGANTIJA	3600 - 3300
	SAFLIENI	3300 - 3000
	TARXIEN	3000 - 2500
BRONZE AGE	TARXIEN CEMETERY	2000 - 1500
	BORG IN-NADUR	1500 - 700
	BAHRIJA	900 - 700
PHOENICIAN-PUNIC	PHOENICIAN	700 - 550
	PUNIC	550 - 218
ROMAN	ROMAN	218 - 535 AD

One episode remains impressed in Maltese tradition - the shipwreck of St. Paul (c. AD 58). To commemorate the event, St. Paul's Square in Rabat was created together with a large statue of the apostle, as a centre for the veneration of the saint in Malta. The legend also speaks of a cave where the apostle lived, now St. Paul's Grotto, over which a chapel has been built, as described in a document dated 1372. In the 18th century, the Church of St. Paul was built. A series of interconnected labyrinthine catacombs extends under the modern town of Rabat. The tombs do not belong only to the Palaeochristian period, but also to the Phoenician and Roman periods, and contain the remains of people of all the religions existing in those times - pagan, Jewish and Christian. The catacombs of St. Paul and St. Agatha are decorated with valuable frescoes.

Ghar Dalam

The discovery of the cave of Ghar Dalam must be credited to the Genoese geologist Professor Arturo Issel (1842-1922).

The professor was carrying out research into the existence of Palaeolithic man in Malta, when he came across the remains of hippopotami in the cave he was exploring, together with a large number of terracotta fragments. This was an obvious indication of the extremely early presence of man on the islands.

Ghar Dalam lies in south-east Malta, near Birzebbuga, and stretches for about 144 metres, scattered with imposing stalagmites and stalactites.

During the Ice Age as a result of the drop in the level of the Mediterranean, Malta was evidently joined to Sicily by a landbridge which allowed animals to migrate there from Europe.

With the successive melting of the ice sheets and the consequent rise in sea levels, the landbridge joining Sicily and Malta disappeared, trapping the European fauna on the archipelago. In order to survive the Maltese environmental conditions, these animals had to evolve, thereby creating breeds of dwarf elephants, hippopotami, brown bears and other mammals.

11

Before you enter the cave, there is a small building. This is home to an interesting museum which is run with efficiency and passion. The museum displays the skeletons of modern-day animals which recall the species that inhabited these islands during the Pleistocene Era.

Above: The temple of Ta' Hagrat from the Skorba phase. Below: The temple of Mgarr.

Ggantija

This was the first prehistoric monument to be excavated and revealed, in 1827. It lies on Malta's twin island, Gozo. The discovery of this site made it possible to date the beginning of the phase which takes its name, that is to say 3600 BC. The site consists of two separate temples lying side by side which, although they share a common surrounding wall, each have their own entrance.

The two temples are known as the Southern Temple and the Northern Temple and although they are similar in shape, their size differs. The Southern Temple is much bigger and contains five apsides. The Northern Temple has a similar layout, but with four apsides and a semicircular niche at the back. The principal building material is coralline limestone. This religious area was in use throughout the Chalcolithic Era (an intermediate phase between the Stone Age and the Bronze Age), or, on Malta, between the Zebbug and Tarxien phases, from 4100 BC to 3000 BC.

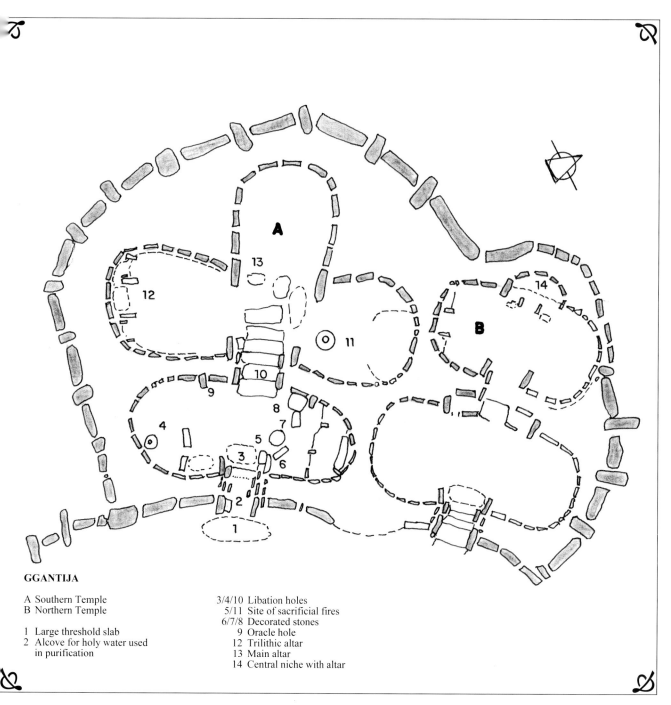

GGANTIJA

A Southern Temple
B Northern Temple

1 Large threshold slab
2 Alcove for holy water used
  in purification

3/4/10 Libation holes
5/11 Site of sacrificial fires
6/7/8 Decorated stones
9 Oracle hole
12 Trilithic altar
13 Main altar
14 Central niche with altar

On these pages, various views of the megalithic complex of Ggantija.

Different views of the Southern and Northern Temples which form the complex of Ggantija.

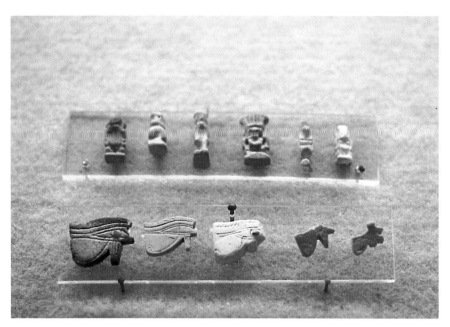

Objects from the various Maltese cultures are displayed in the archaeological museum in Vittoria (Gozo). Of particular note is a tombstone in Kufic characters dating from 1174.

Hagar Qim

The name Hagar Qim would appear to mean "erect stones". The megalithic complex of Hagar Qim, along with the temples of Mnajdra, is one of the most important religious centres of the southern half of the island of Malta. Built with globigerina limestone, the Hagar Qim complex consists of four edifices. The biggest, known as the Southern Temple, is situated at the centre of the complex. Beside it is the Northern Temple. To the east of the Southern Temple lies an important religious building together with the ruins of a fourth temple. It was in the Southern Temple that the obese statuettes were found. These are now on display at the Museum of Archaeology in Valletta.

The Hagar Qim complex belongs to the Tarxien phase, the apex of the Temple Culture period, which covers the years from 3000 BC to 2500 BC.

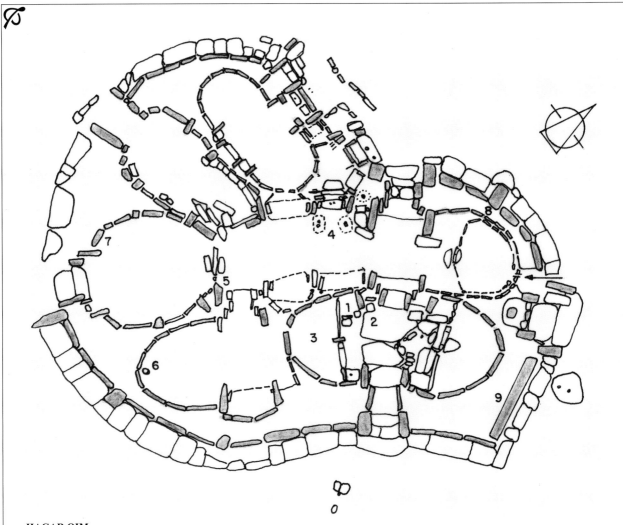

HAGAR QIM

1 Altar with floral decorations
2 Stone shelf with decorations
3 Discovery site of Maltese Venus
4 Mushroom-shaped altar
5 Discovery site of numerous figurines, in 1945

6 Cylindrical pilaster
7 Fragments of carved stone figures
8 Largest stone in the complex
9 Largest stone used in construction of temples

Mnajdra

The megalithic site of Mnajdra consists of two temples which lie side by side without being connected, each with its own entrance. The site also includes a separate religious building and the remains of various other megalithic structures. The entire complex is situated approximately 500 metres towards the sea from Hagar Qim and lies in an open area of globigerina, with a spectacular view of the sea and the tiny island of Filfla. The Mnajdra complex, built in hard coralline limestone, is one of the oldest religious sites of the Temple Culture period.

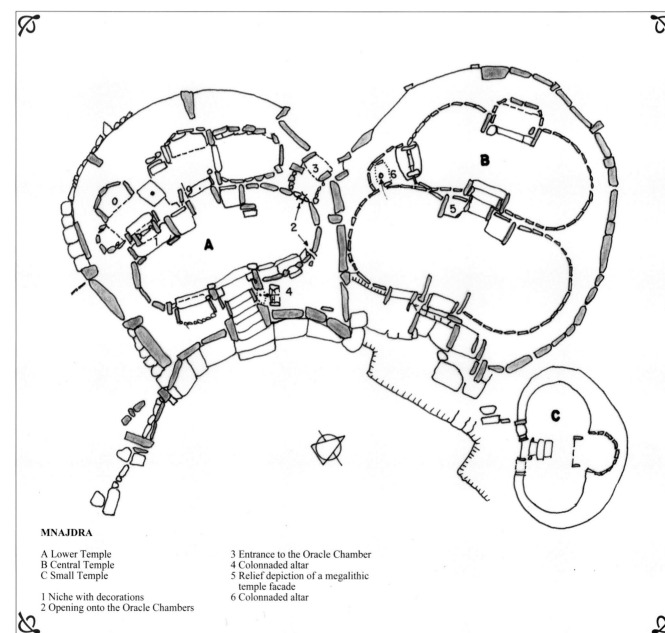

MNAJDRA

A Lower Temple
B Central Temple
C Small Temple

1 Niche with decorations
2 Opening onto the Oracle Chambers

3 Entrance to the Oracle Chamber
4 Colonnaded altar
5 Relief depiction of a megalithic
  temple facade
6 Colonnaded altar

Different views of the Mnajdra complex, which consists of two temples.

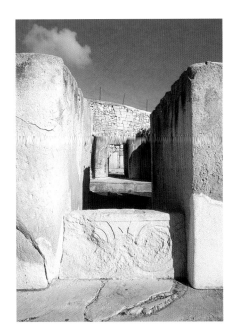

The Tarxien Temples

It was the father of Maltese archaeology, Sir Themistocles Zammit, who defined Hal Tarxien as a complex consisting of three connected temples with a fourth near the Eastern Temple, as reported by Joachim von Freeden. It is from this group that the Tarxien phase takes its name, a phase which begins in 3000 BC and continues up to about 2500 BC. This phase stands out for the highly evolved aspect which megalithic temple construction had reached. The three temples - First, Second and Third - are joined to each other by passages and are enclosed by the same surrounding wall. Beside the First Temple are the scattered remains of an older fourth temple, the last vestiges of its existence.

This religious complex was in continuous use from the Zebbug phase throughout the Temple Culture period.

HAL TARXIEN

A First (Western) Temple
B Second (Central) Temple
C Third (Eastern) Temple
D Original temple

1 Oracle stone
2 Colossal stone idol
3/4/5 Altars decorated with spirals
6 Animal forms in relief

7 Discovery site of most decorated stone
8 Ancient casket
9 Stone container
10 Animal forms in relief
11 Highly-polished stone shelves, decorated with spirals
12 Stone balls used for transporting blocks
13 Apse and oracle chamber
14 Limekiln

Excavation work on the Bronze Age complex of Tarxien began in 1914. Apart from a colossal statue, of which there remains only the lower portion, the complex has produced valuable stone slabs decorated with relief friezes of geometric motifs or series of animals.

HYPOGEUM OF HAL SAFLIENI

1 New entrance
2 Modern-day cistern
3 Main chamber
4 Passage with trilithic system
5 Unfinished chamber
6 Oracle Chamber
7 Second decorated room
8 Anima cavity
9 Holy of Holies
10 Treasury
11 Passage leading to lower level
12 Slope leading to a raised part
13 Remains of a trilithic door
14 Bone recess
15 Passage leading to upper level
16 Trilithic door
17 Neolithic burial place
18 Neolithic cistern
19 Original entrance

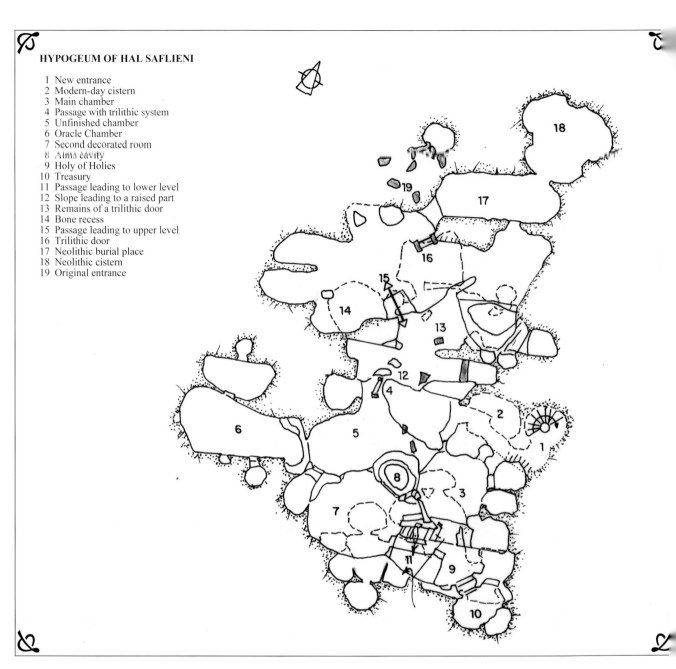

al Saflieni

al Saflieni, otherwise known as
the Hypogeum of Paola (from the
Greek "ipogeion"), is a subterranean place of worship. It was
discovered by chance in 1902.
Excavation work under the
supervision of Sir Themistocles
Zammit began in 1905 and continued for six years.

The Hypogeum, which was carved
out of the globigerina limestone,
occupies a vast underground area
and was used as a sepulchre and
place of worship. The complex
extends over three underground
levels and creates an impression
of vastness. The chambers repeat
the same architectural elements
as those of the open-air temples,
only carved out of the subterranean rock.

On the second level lies the
"Oracle Chamber" which has a
ceiling decorated with ochre-
coloured spirals on the globigerina surface. Another architectural-
ly important room is the "Holy of
Holies", valued for its refinements. The so-called "Painted
Chamber" too is famous for its
decorations. The walls, from the
floor up to a height of about 4 ft,
are decorated with large, red,
painted spirals, and the ceiling
with wonderful frescoes.

The entire surface area of the
complex measures 2,500 square
metres.

Top: Statuette of a human figure lying.
Bottom: Woman's head in limestone.
Both of these were discovered during
excavations at the Hypogeum of Paola.
Next page: The Dolmen of Naxxar.

37

As in other parts of the ancient Mediterranean world, the spread of Christianity brought with it the excavation and creation of catacombs in order to escape Roman persecution. The catacombs served as secret meeting places for worship and for the burial of the dead, as the Christian belief in the resurrection of the body necessitated conservation of corpses. The great respect for the dead can be seen in the frescoes and sculptures which decorate these tombs. On these pages are some images of the Salina catacombs.

Above: Aerial view of Mdina, which together with Rabat, lies over the ancient towns of Gaudos and Melita.
Below: The entrance to the Museum of Roman Antiquities in Rabat and on the next page, some Roman remains on display at the museum.

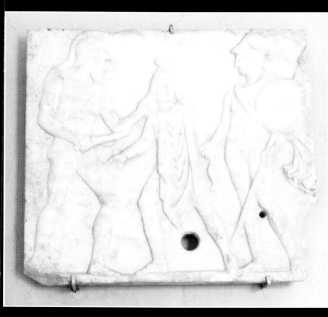

This page: The beautiful floor mosaic of the inner courtyard in the museum.
Next page: Details from some other Roman mosaics.

43

Various objects from the Roman period on display at the museum. Next page, bottom right: Stone olive press.

46

*Some views of the baths at Ghajn
Tuffieha, evidence of the Roman
presence on Malta.*

On these two pages: The crypt of the
Church of St. Agatha in Rabat with the
beautiful frescoes from the Early
Christian period.

Views of the catacombs of St. Paul in Rabat. The arrival of the Apostle marked the beginning of the evangelization of Malta.

The National Museum of Archaeology

The home of the National Museum of Archaeology the Auberge de Provence, in Valletta. The Auberge, once home to the knights of the French langue, was designed and built by the Maltese architect Girolamo Cassar, in 1574.

Recently renovated, the home of the National Museum of Archaeology exhibits archaeological finds from various digs in an attractive and elegant way. The exhibits are drawn from all the various periods of history, from Neolithic to Roman. Among the most interesting pieces on display is the famous " Maltese Venus " and the equally renowned "Sleeping Lady" which was found in the Hypogeum of Hal Saflieni at Paola, not forgetting the mysterious fat figures from Hagar Qim. Finally there is also an interesting collection of bas-reliefs from the temples, pottery, utensils and Roman and Punic coins.

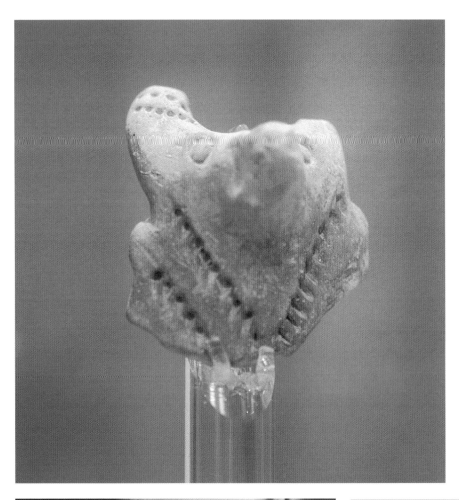

Left: Clay animal's head with decorations typical of the Ghar Dalam phase. Below: Clay utensil, fragments and pottery from the Grey and Red Skorba phases. Next page: Some objects from the Zebbug phase - above, the sculpted stone represents a human face. Below left: Terracotta fragment with incised human figure. Right: Vase with handle. and incised decorations.

From the temple of Bugibba, stone slab with decorations representing fish and below, slab with spirals in relief.

Bas-reliefs of animals and terracotta statue from the complex at Tarxien.

Limestone figure from Hagar Qim with typical obese features and indeterminate sex. Next page: Original stone altar decorated with floral motifs on all four sides, a copy of which can be seen at Hagar Qim. Above right: The Maltese Venus. Below: The Sleeping Lady, found in the Hypogeum of Hal Saflieni.

Stone sculpture from a Punic tomb at Qallilija. Below: Tombstone with Puni[c] inscription and Sign of Tanit. Bottom o[f] page: Terracotta masks from the 6th and 5th centuries BC, discovered in Punic tombs.

GLOSSARY

Apse: A semicircular recess at the end of a building or nave.

Atrium: The central courtyard of ancient Roman houses, often surrounded by a colonnade.

Catacomb: An underground burial place used by early Christians to escape from persecution during the first centuries A.D.

Dolmen: From the Old Breton dol ("table") and men ("smooth stone"). A megalithic monument consisting of several upright stones supporting a large, flat, horizontal roofing stone.

Doric: An archaic architectural order, originating in Greece.

Graffito: An inscription or drawing effected by carving or scratching cave walls, stone or terracotta.

Holy of Holies: The most sacred area of a temple or other place of worship.

Hypogeum: A subterranean building, used as a place of worship or as a burial place.

Langue: One of the eight 16th century divisions of the knights of St. John in Malta based on native language, each with its own duties and Auberge, or headquarters.

Menhir: A large, tall stone set into the ground. Generally roughly square, some menhirs also present refinements. They are sometimes arranged in line and are thought to be religious symbols or funerary monuments for certain Neolithic peoples.

Municipium: A town under Roman control which was granted a degree of self-administration without the full political rights of Rome.

Obsidian: A volcanic rock, usually black and glassy. Used in the Neolithic period for cutting implements and weapon points.

Peristyle: A colonnade surrounding a building or courtyard.

Tetrastyle temple: A greek temple supported by four frontal or lateral columns.

Triclinium: The dining room of a Roman house furnished with three wide couches arranged around three sides of the room. People ate while lying on their left-hand side.

Trilithic system: An arrangement of stone blocks with a large horizontal block supported by two vertical blocks which create a sort of stone table.

Vestibule: A small anteroom which leads to a larger room or hall.

Wied: A valley formed along the bed of a river which is now dried up.

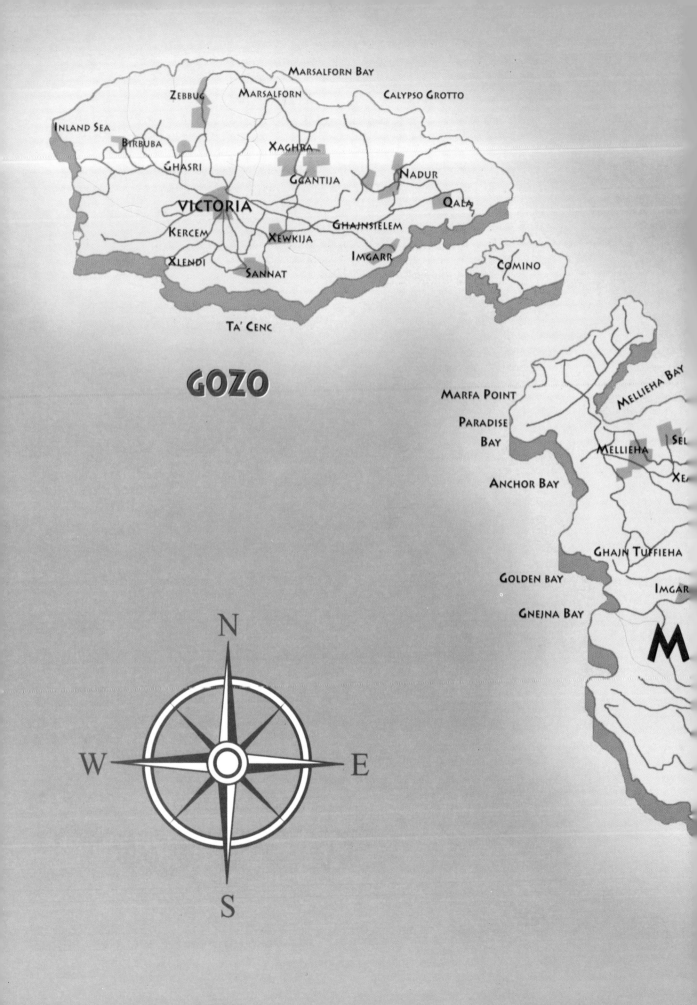

GOZO

MARSALFORN BAY

ZEBBUĠ
MARSALFORN
CALYPSO GROTTO

INLAND SEA
BIRBUBA
XAGĦRA
ĠĦASRI
ĠGANTIJA
NADUR
VICTORIA
QALA
KERĊEM
ĠĦAJNSIELEM
XEWKIJA
COMINO
XLENDI
IMĠARR
SANNAT

TA' ĊENĊ

MARFA POINT
MELLIEĦA BAY
PARADISE
BAY
MELLIEĦA
SEL
XE
ANCHOR BAY

ĠĦAJN TUFFIEĦA

GOLDEN BAY
IMGAR
GNEJNA BAY
M

N
W   E
S

REPUBLIC OF MALTA

ISLAND

UL'S BAY

SALINA BAY

AWL IL-BAHAR

ST. JULIAN'S

MARSAMXETT
HARBOUR

SLIEMA

VALLETTA

GZIRA

NAXXAR

MSIDA

MOSTA

FLORIANA

VITTORIOSA

BIRKIRKARA

COSPICUA

SANTA VENERA

TA

HAMRUN

ZABBAR

ATTARD

QORMI

PAOLA

MARSASKALA

MDINA

HAL TARXIEN

ZEBBUG

LUQA

ZEJTUN

ST. THOMAS BAY

RABAT

TAS-SILG

GHAXAQ

GLI

MARSAXLOKK

SIGGIEWI

LUQA AIRPORT

BUSKETT GARDENS

MQABBA

KIRKOP

BIRZEBBUGIA

MARSAXLOKK
BAY

DELIMARA POINT

QRENDI

ZURRIEQ

BLUE GROTTO

Index

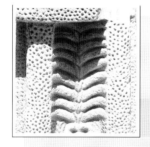

Photographs by: Bruna Polimeni

Cover Design by:Enzo Sferra

Translation by: Merven J. Grealey

The publishers would like to thank the following for their kind assistance:
Dr Mark Anthony Mifsud of the National Museum of Archaeology, Valletta
Dr George Zammit Maempel, curator of Ghar Dalam.

Picture on page 35 (top) from "MALTA" of Joachim Von Freeden, published by Darmstadt publisher.

Printed in the EU by I.G.E.R. - Rome